WISDOM IN
NONSENSE

HEATHER O'NEILL

CLC KREISEL LECTURE SERIES

WISDOM IN NONSENSE

INVALUABLE LESSONS FROM MY FATHER

The University of Alberta Press

Published by

The University of Alberta Press
Ring House 2
Edmonton, Alberta, Canada T6G 2E1
www.uap.ualberta.ca
and
Canadian Literature Centre /
Centre de littérature canadienne
3–5 Humanities Centre
University of Alberta
Edmonton, Alberta, Canada T6G 2E5
www.abclc.ca

Copyright © 2018 Heather O'Neill
Introduction © 2018 Kit Dobson

LIBRARY AND ARCHIVES CANADA
CATALOGUING IN PUBLICATION

O'Neill, Heather, 1973–, author
      Wisdom in nonsense : invaluable lessons
from my father / Heather O'Neill.

(CLC Kreisel lecture series)
Issued in print and electronic formats.
Co-published by Canadian Literature Centre.
ISBN 978-1-77212-377-7 (softcover).—
ISBN 978-1-77212-400-2 (EPUB).—
ISBN 978-1-77212-401-9 (Kindle).—
ISBN 978-1-77212-399-9 (PDF)

      1. O'Neill, Heather, 1973– —Childhood and
youth. 2. Authors, Canadian (English)—20th
century—Biography. 3. Fathers and daughters—
Canada—Biography. I. Canadian Literature Centre,
issuing body II. Title. III. Series: CLC Kreisel
lecture series

PS8579.N387Z46 2018   C813'.54
C2017-907090-8

First edition, second printing, 2018.
Printed and bound in Canada by Houghton Boston
Printers, Saskatoon, Saskatchewan.
Copyediting and proofreading by Peter Midgley.

The University of Alberta Press is committed to
protecting our natural environment. As part of
our efforts, this book is printed on Enviro Paper: it
contains 100% post-consumer recycled fibres and
is acid- and chlorine-free.

The Canadian Literature Centre acknowledges
the support of the Alberta Foundation for the Arts
for the CLC Kreisel Lecture delivered by Heather
O'Neill in March 2017 at the University of Alberta.

The University of Alberta Press gratefully acknowledges the support received for its publishing
program from the Government of Canada, the
Canada Council for the Arts, and the Government
of Alberta through the Alberta Media Fund.

CONTENTS

FOREWORD | *The CLC Kreisel Lecture Series*

HERE WE ARE with the eleventh annual CLC Kreisel Lecture, delivered on March 9, 2017, at the University of Alberta. Anglo-Quebecker novelist, Heather O'Neill, joins ten other authors in a series which continues to realize most fully the Canadian Literature Centre's mission: to bring together writers, readers, students, researchers, and teachers in an open, inclusive, and critical forum focused on Canada's literary arts. The Kreisel Series showcases a myriad of issues, at times painful, at times joyful, but always salient and far-reaching: social justice, cultural identity, place and displacement, the spoils of history, storytelling, censorship, language, and reading in a digital age. In these pages, Heather O'Neill's lecture, an event headed this year by Acting CLC Director Daniel Laforest, presents personal reflections about growing up in an underworld of Montreal's Plateau Mont-Royal, a setting that also vividly crops up in O'Neill's fiction. Led through this world of little criminals, street performers, and drug addicts by her bad advice–wielding father, she depicts an oddly happy childhood and the wise tenderness of a daughter's reminiscences. The Kreisel Series confronts questions that concern us all within the specificities of our contemporary experience, whatever our differences. O'Neill's lecture epitomizes, with thoughtfulness and depth as well as humour and grace, the spirit of free and honest dialogue that characterizes the series.

These public lectures also set out to honour Professor Henry Kreisel's legacy in an annual public forum. Author, University Professor and Officer of the Order of Canada, Henry Kreisel was born in Vienna into a Jewish family in 1922. He left his homeland for England in 1938 and was interned in Canada for eighteen months during the Second World War. After studying at the University of Toronto, he began teaching in 1947 at the University of Alberta, and served as Chair of English from 1961 until 1970. He served as Vice-President (Academic) from 1970 to 1975, and was named University Professor in 1975, the highest scholarly award bestowed on its faculty members by the University of Alberta. Professor Kreisel was an inspiring and beloved teacher who taught generations of students to love literature and was one of the first people to bring the immigrant experience to modern Canadian literature. He died in Edmonton in 1991. His works include two novels, *The Rich Man* (1948) and *The Betrayal* (1964), and a collection of short stories, *The Almost Meeting* (1981). His internment diary, alongside critical essays on his writing, appears in *Another Country: Writings By and About Henry Kreisel* (1985).

The generosity of Professor Kreisel's teaching at the University of Alberta profoundly inspires the CLC in its public outreach, research pursuits, and continued commitment to the ever-growing richness and diversity of Canada's writings. The Centre embraces Henry Kreisel's pioneering focus on the knowledge of one's own literatures. It is in his memory that we seek to foster a better understanding of a complicated, difficult world, which literature can help us reimagine and even transform.

The Canadian Literature Centre was established in 2006, thanks to the leadership gift of the noted Edmontonian bibliophile, Dr. Eric Schloss.

MARIE CARRIÈRE
Director, Canadian Literature Centre
Edmonton, September 2017

LIMINAIRE | *La collection des Conférences Kreisel du CLC*

VOICI LA onzième Conférence Kreisel annuelle du CLC, présentée le 9 mars 2017 à l'Université de l'Alberta. La romancière anglo-québécoise, Heather O'Neill, vient rejoindre les dix autres auteurs d'une collection qui réalise à son plus fort la mission du Centre de littérature canadienne: celle de rassembler écrivains et écrivaines, lecteurs et lectrices, étudiants et étudiantes, chercheurs et chercheuses, enseignants et enseignantes, dans un forum ouvert, inclusif et critique consacré aux arts littéraires du Canada. La Collection Kreisel met en valeur de nombreuses problématiques, parfois douloureuses, parfois joyeuses, or toujours saillantes et considérables: la justice sociale, l'identité culturelle, le lieu et le déplacement, les dépouilles de l'histoire, la narration, la censure, le langage et la lecture à l'ère numérique. Présidée par le directeur intérimaire du CLC cette année, Daniel Laforest, la conférence de Heather O'Neill dans ces pages nous montre la jeune écrivaine grandir dans une pègre du Plateau Mont-Royal à Montréal, un lieu également présent dans les textes fictifs de l'auteure. Conduite dans ce monde de petits délinquants par un père brandissant une abondance de mauvais conseils, elle dépeint une enfance curieusement heureuse et la sage tendresse des souvenirs d'une fille de son père. La Collection Kreisel s'affronte aux questions qui nous concernent tous et toutes selon les spécificités de notre vécu contemporain, peu importent nos différences. Dans une intention de dialogue libre et honnête, elle se produit, à l'exemple de O'Neill ici, dans l'ardeur et la profondeur intellectuelles ainsi que l'humour et l'élégance.

Ces conférences publiques et annuelles se consacrent à perpétuer la mémoire du Professeur Henry Kreisel. Auteur, professeur universitaire et Officier de l'Ordre du Canada, Henry Kreisel est né à Vienne d'une famille juive en 1922. En 1938, il a quitté son pays natal pour l'Angleterre et a été interné pendant dix-huit mois, au Canada, lors de la Deuxième Guerre mondiale. Après ses études à l'Université de Toronto, il devint professeur à l'Université de l'Alberta en 1947, et à partir de 1961 jusqu'à 1970, il a dirigé le Département d'anglais. De 1970 à 1975, il a été vice-recteur (universitaire), et a été nommé professeur hors rang en 1975, la plus haute distinction scientifique décernée par l'Université de l'Alberta à un membre de son professorat. Professeur adoré, il a transmis l'amour de la littérature à plusieurs générations d'étudiants, et il a été parmi les premiers écrivains modernes du Canada à aborder l'expérience immigrante. Il est décédé à Edmonton en 1991. Son œuvre comprend les romans, *The Rich*

Man (1948) et *The Betrayal* (1964), et un recueil de nouvelles intitulé *The Almost Meeting* (1981). Son journal d'internement, accompagné d'articles critiques sur ses écrits, paraît dans *Another Country: Writings By and About Henry Kreisel* (1985).

La générosité du Professeur Kreisel est une source d'inspiration profonde quant au travail public et scientifique du CLC de sonder la grande diversité et la qualité remarquable des écrits du Canada. Le Centre adhère à l'importance qu'accordait de façon inaugurale Henry Kreisel à la connaissance des littératures de son propre pays. C'est à sa mémoire que nous poursuivons une meilleure compréhension d'un monde compliqué et difficile que la littérature peut nous aider à imaginer et transformer.

Le Centre de littérature canadienne a été créé en 2006 grâce au don directeur du bibliophile illustre edmontonien, le docteur Eric Schloss.

MARIE CARRIÈRE
Directrice, Centre de littérature canadienne
Edmonton, septembre 2017

INTRODUCTION

WHEN I WAS ASKED to introduce Heather O'Neill, I felt both lucky and fortunate. Yet also challenged. Heather O'Neill is someone who can be introduced based on her achievements alone: she is the author of three jaw-droppingly good novels—*Lullabies for Little Criminals*, *The Girl Who Was Saturday Night*, and 2017's *The Lonely Hearts Hotel*—as well as the short story collection *Daydreams of Angels* and the collection of poems *two eyes are you sleeping*. Her work has won Canada Reads, the Hugh MacLennan Prize, and the Danuta Gleed Literary Award, and has been on the short- and long-lists for many top national and international literary prizes including the Giller Prize, the Governor General's Award, and the IMPAC Dublin Literary Award. The accolades are mounting up and, I will wager, are only going to continue with the publication of her new work.

But an introduction of this sort sells Heather's achievements short, at least in my view. Heather O'Neill's writing is difficult and challenging, yet beautiful and soothing. To focus on her novels, in particular, might allow us to see what

I mean. Her first novel, *Lullabies for Little Criminals* (2006), features Baby, a girl who lives in central Montreal. She spends her time wandering through the Plateau neighbourhood, her eyes full of the wonder and curiosity that can characterize young people just coming into themselves. She is remarkably open to the world, fantastically perceptive, and as troublesome as can be. The world of wonders in which Baby lives, however, is a frightening one to read about from this side of adolescence, as we watch her father's battle with his addiction continue to worsen and, as no one maintains much interest in guiding her, the neighbourhood pimp begins to take his own, far from benevolent, interest. Throughout *Lullabies*, Heather presents us with a doubled vision: that which Baby manages somehow to maintain, one that hangs on to childhood despite terrible circumstances; and that which the reader brings to the text, full of concern for the wayward protagonist and wary of each of her troubling choices.

Heather's subsequent novel, *The Girl Who Was Saturday Night*, published in 2014, returns us to the Plateau in Montreal, this time to the era of the second referendum in Quebec, the 1995 vote that narrowly resulted in Quebec's remaining a part of Canada. O'Neill's protagonist, Nouschka, and her brother, Nicolas, are the children of a once famous, now failed and disgraced, fictional singer associated with the Quebec sovereignty movement. Nouschka and Nicolas experience a youth filled with rash acts, discover sex through others in the neighbourhood, and struggle to survive in their impoverished surroundings as a documentary film crew descends upon them, seeking to make a film about their dysfunctional family. Here again, the Plateau, and the boulevard St-Laurent in particular, is a site of unusual assortments, of people who hang around smoking their cigarettes in impossible weather and who offer Nouschka and Nicolas worrying openings to adulthood. The novel is brimful of a feeling of wasted decadence, of risk, and of cats. O'Neill's writing is always, it seems, full of cats and of characters who are tragically flawed, yet who are nonetheless honest and true.

Her new novel, *The Lonely Hearts Hotel*, is again set in Montreal, but this time readers find themselves in the historical Montreal of the Depression. *The Lonely Hearts Hotel* stars the orphaned children Rose and Pierrot, who, after being raised in the same orphanage, struggle to find their way in Montreal's underworld, a place populated by gangsters, mistresses, sex workers, addicts—and clowns. Rose and Pierrot retain their whimsy and charm despite a world that would harden them, that would harm them, and that, at times, would eliminate them entirely. The turn in this novel to a more historical focus is something that interests me greatly, but I am, above all else, deeply compelled by her characters. For it is her characters who are difficult, challenging, beautiful, and soothing. This combination is not an easy one to maintain.

Reading O'Neill's work is like eating ice cream on a hot summer's day: even if you don't want to do so, even if you wish to savour it, you have to rush, you have to go at it with gusto and abandon, lest it melt all over you. Her books read like melting ice cream. If that simile seems a bit laboured, and it probably is, that's in part because my own similes simply cannot keep up with O'Neill's. Similes leap from her pages, and I find myself anticipating the next outrageously perfect one. There are so many to choose from, but I will limit myself to one example from early on in her new novel:

XVIII

> *Rose and Pierrot were orphans. There was something magical about hearing them talk about their tragic circumstances in such high-pitched voices. They were metaphors for sadness. It was like someone playing a requiem on a xylophone. It wasn't something you heard every day. (Lonely 36)*[1]

"Like someone playing a requiem on a xylophone": a perfect simile, but one that needs everything that comes before it, the sweep of the narrative and the metaphor, to bring into relief the dissonant contrast between the form of the requiem and the utterly inadequate instrument of the xylophone. The clash is both funny and sad. Again and again, her paragraphs soar to the point of the simile, to the moment where everything is revealed through a comparison that forces readers to pause and to recognize precisely what a driving force is at work in this writing.

For these reasons and more, I find myself thinking about Heather's writing in my own modest endeavours. Last year, I had the tremendous privilege of living in Montreal, in the heart of the Plateau that Heather's work describes so beautifully. I was there with my family, in part, to write about the city. We spent our time gathering fragments of whimsy, which we found in every direction we turned. Learning the meaning of the word "whimsy," in fact, was a very important part of conversations with my two daughters. We watched acrobats practicing in the park, saw unicyclists pushing forward into blizzards, said hellos to cats walking along fence tops, and noticed a steady stream of university students in oversized sunglasses eating ice cream on the street corners. Every weekend brought a new festival, and the street art was as fantastic as the galleries, even if the roads were sometimes impassable due to construction, due to ice, or due to street parties. It is a city that Heather's writing captures magnificently, and that I enjoyed all the more for reading her works while I was there.

As I close my introduction, I think that it is worth noting a small but perhaps important coincidence. This year marks the eleventh CLC Kreisel Lecture. The number eleven is a magical number in *The Lonely Hearts Hotel*, popping up at important junctures. The number eleven serves as a code between Rose and Pierrot: it is their default number, and the age at which they both agree that they were the happiest. Perhaps this time, this eleventh occasion of this lecture, may be among our happiest too.

KIT DOBSON
Edmonton, March 2017

Work cited

1. O'Neill, Heather. *The Lonely Hearts Hotel*. HarperCollins, 2017.

PRELUDE

WHEN I WAS FIVE YEARS OLD, my parents got divorced. My mother packed me up and put me in the back seat of our burgundy car. She tossed my dad's stuff out of the trunk and we drove down to Virginia. After two and a half years of moving around, she told me she had changed her mind about wanting to be my mother. She put me on a plane and I showed up back in Montreal.

My dad was a petty criminal as a child. He worked sneaking into windows for older hardened cons and was in prison for a year when he was eleven years old. As an adult, he worked as a janitor, but he saw himself as street smart. He had a little silver transistor radio that he attached to his belt and which kept him abreast of the news. He listened to it so often that he assumed that he was as intelligent as the most intelligent people were.

My dad was determined to take care of me properly. He made pancakes and cookies and sewed my clothes. He was actually really good at that. He was a little worse at what he regarded as an integral part of parenting: the dispensing of life advice. But, nonetheless, it was one of his favourite things to do.

He liked spending time with me because I had to look up to him. I was only seven. He treated me as though I was his junior partner. He had several rules that he was adamant about.

I HAD BEEN GIVEN A JOURNAL when I was eight years old by my mother's brother. I quite liked books of all types, but here was one filled with empty pages, waiting for me to put the words in it. I loved the feeling of chronicling my daily adventures in the black journal. It made the events of my life seem important and worthy of a novel.

My dad insisted I knock it off. He told me that it was a terrible habit because everything that one wrote in a diary was ultimately used against a person in court. He thought of being tried in court as a rite of passage everyone went through at one point in life.

I wonder whether he felt exposed. I wonder if it made him feel as though he were under surveillance. As though I would be able to return to these journals as an adult and then judge what he had done and his behaviour. But, no matter how many journals he threw out, I would continue to write in them. I'm writing in one now.

LESSON 2 | *Learn to Play the Tuba*

MY DAD INSISTED that when I got to high school I play the tuba. He said the world didn't have enough tuba players, and, thus, there would always be a shortage. You could always get a job if you played the tuba.

I was very worried about being able to earn a living. If I was just allowed to play the tuba in music class, my problems would already be over at eleven.

The girls in my class told me I was too skinny to play the tuba and it was always given to the fattest kid. I was sure I could hold it. I thought it would be like having a baby elephant in my lap all the time. And that seemed like a good thing. I looked at the tuba with longing and desire, as though it were a fat millionaire in a tailored suit who could take care of me for the rest of my life.

But there was only one tuba, and it was given to a really big boy. I, instead, was given a trumpet as my instrument. I wept playing the trumpet for the first three months. The teacher said there was a peculiar sadness to the way I played the trumpet. I earned an A in music class, although I didn't think I deserved it.

LESSON 3 | *Never Share Your Scientific Research*

I TOLD MY DAD how in class we were allowed to choose a partner for a project on the solar system. My dad lost it. He said that my partner would steal my research and pass it off as their own. They would go on to be famous and I would be penniless. So, reluctantly, I told the teacher that I didn't want to have a partner.

But I didn't feel good about it at all. All the information that I got about Jupiter, I had copied pretty much directly from the set of encyclopedias that were on the shelf in the school library.

These were facts that were available to everybody. I wasn't going to be making any great breakthroughs about the planet that a partner could win the Nobel Prize with.

One of my favourite segments on *The Muppet Show* was "Pigs in Space." It seemed so much fun to go into outer space. It would be like you got to go on a sleepover party that lasted for three years and wear your pyjamas all the time and eat TV dinners. It wouldn't be in the least enjoyable alone. Especially not if you encountered alien life forms.

I saw myself on a planet filling up empty jam jars with sample mushrooms and snails, while eight quadrillion stars turned on and off over my head. The Little Prince had tried a bachelor lifestyle on his planet, and he ended up going mad and entering into a sado-masochistic relationship with a rose.

You had to share your research, I decided. I teamed up with a girl named Lola.

She had a photocopy machine at her house. I was infatu-ated with that machine. I loved when the teacher handed out newly photocopied pages. I would smell them as though they were crack. It was like marker but not marker. Lola photocopied things for me, and I watched the light of the machine move back and forth as though it were the aurora borealis.

Even if she did turn against me and take credit for my ideas about Jupiter, being betrayed was better than being alone.

LESSON 4 | *Make Friends with Jewish Kids*

ANOTHER ONE of my dad's commandments was that I hang out and pay attention to what Jewish kids were doing.

He grew up in a working-class neighbourhood that was filled with French-Canadian and Jewish kids. The Jewish kids had lived in apartments next to him. They had come out to play with him in their pea caps and dirty undershirts. They had swum in the river and cursed and laughed together.

The Jews all went to high school and university. They all left the neighbourhood and did interesting things with their lives. The Jews who had grown up during the Depression were a marvellous and magical upwardly mobile class. While the Jewish kids he grew up with were now running their own companies and factories, he was pretty much where he started off. They had somehow gotten ahead of him. So he was adamant that I always do what the Jewish kids were doing, as they were on their way to great places.

I had a great friend named Malachi when I was nine. He wore Adidas shorts and gym socks up to his knees. He bought a CB radio and would stay up late chatting with truck drivers, who generally had a lot of time on their hands. He was saving all his paper route money because he really wanted to go to therapy. He liked the idea of it. He asked his parents and they said that they weren't paying for it because there was nothing wrong with him.

We spent a lot of time sitting at the bottom of the swimming pool wearing goggles and looking at each other.

I also became friends with a Jewish girl named Mindy. She came to school wearing only tights and a T-shirt, as she believed wearing a skirt was merely ornamental. She had red hair and a perfectly round face. She always reminded me of the ladies in medieval paintings who wagged their fingers at dragons. She wanted to be an actress when she grew up, so she would practice talking as loud as she could. I would stand at the opposite side of the schoolyard and try to hear her.

I'm not exactly sure that I learned anything about success from hanging out with my Jewish friends, but they were some of the most wonderful pals I ever had.

LESSON 5 | *Accept That You're Ugly and Move On*

MY FATHER SAID when I was a baby, I was so ugly that he was afraid to look at me. He would close his eyes and say, no, she can't be that ugly. But then when he opened them, there I was, even uglier than he remembered. He said my eyes looked like they were jumping out of my head. He was so embarrassed at the hospital when the nurse held me up for him to take a peek. When he rode the bus home with me in his arms, he put a blanket over my head, so as not to shock anyone.

He said that when I cried, the most frightening howl came out of my mouth. Once there was an alley cat on the fire escape, trying to get through the window, having mistaken me for one of its own. He had to throw a glass of water at it. Sometimes I like to imagine that cat with a bouquet of flowers in its paw and a bowtie around its neck, knocking on the window, looking for me.

As a child, he told me he was afraid a wind would pick me up and carry me away because my ears were so large. He said that I didn't really need to take a bus to school. All I had to do was hold up my hair in a ponytail, and I could use my ears to fly there like Dumbo.

He called me Chicken Legs as an affectionate nickname. Because he said I was so skinny.

I grew up thinking I was butt ugly. It was kind of nice, thinking I was ugly. It made me feel that I had to work on my other attributes. It took off the pressure of even trying to look good. I wore an old fedora and second-hand clothes as I rode my bicycle around the neighbourhood. The boys always mocked me because of how I acted and dressed. It was because I didn't care. I just didn't care what they thought of me.

Often little girls are bombarded with praise for their superficial qualities and are informed, from the time they can understand a sentence, what the male gaze thinks of them. Being beautiful is only conforming most perfectly to an ideal. I always liked the idea of being unique. If I could be the ugliest baby in the whole city, then that seemed like an accomplishment.

LESSON 6 | *Never Tell Anyone What Your Parents Do for a Living*

MY DAD TOLD ME that I should never tell anyone what my parents did for a living. He said it was no one's business. He said that they would judge me, and never give me any opportunities in life.

On my birth certificate, under "Occupation," my father wrote that he was a Professor of Philosophy.

Having dropped out in Grade Three, my father's reading skills were rather limited. He got me to read everything that came in the mail out loud to him, so it might seem an outrageous lie to claim that he was a professor of philosophy. But the lie wasn't completely out of left field. He did tend to pontificate, and his friends did tend to listen to what he said, and contemplate his conclusions and assumptions. I think that lying is just a way of telling the truth in a metaphorical way.

In elementary school, I always had to fill out a form with parental information. He told me to tell the teacher that he was a spy and therefore all the required information was classified. The gym teacher asked me if it was true that my father was a spy. I looked down at my burgundy running shoes. "I'm not at liberty to say," I responded.

When I enrolled in high school, my father listed his profession as Sculptor. That year he had a job as a janitor for a building. The fence around the building came down. He had been collecting broken hockey sticks outside the skating rink for years. He sawed the blades off the hockey sticks and screwed them together. Everyone stopped and stared at the new fence he had constructed. He had probably lowered the property value by a hundred thousand dollars in one morning. But occasionally one of the viewers would exclaim, "This is quite marvellous." It was a true objet d'art.

By teaching me to lie about who I was, my dad instilled in me the notion that the differences were actually superficial. They were just outward trappings. And if you were to change coats with a rich person, then you would immediately become one.

In life there will always be someone trying to take your personhood away. Someone trying to get you to think you are less than they are. It happens with colour, it happens with gender, it happens with class, it happens with education. There are people who will have you believe that class is hereditary. That you are less of a person.

I was a child of a janitor, but he wanted me to be treated like the child of a professor of philosophy.

LESSON 7 | *Know About Art History*

MY DAD WAS A HOARDER. He always came home with pockets full of objects he had found in the garbage. There's a certain relationship that poor people have with their belongings, a tenderness. Because they have nothing of value, they bequeath a value onto plain objects, and this in turn makes them cherished. It was not the object, but what it symbolized, what it was supposed to be.

Let me elaborate. My dad would give everything a back story. According to him, he had travelled all of Europe after the Second World War to get many of the objects in our apartment. There was a bell jar filled with a plastic rose that he bought from a beautiful girl in Liverpool. He said my reading lamp had come from a woman in Dublin who had one eye and wore compression gym socks, and had an adult child who suffered from ulcers and couldn't work. She had to sell her lamp to support him.

He told me that he learned to make pork chops in a five-star restaurant in Paris. He was a top chef there and would have to make seven dishes at once. There were escargots climbing all over the walls and sad frogs housed in glass jars. He once set a frog free by flushing it down the toilet and wishing it godspeed. And he had brought home our utensils from there.

It seemed irrelevant whether these stories were true or not, as I loved listening to them. He never let anything be ordinary. Everything around me, from the doorknob to the lamp was splendid with meaning and belonged in a museum. I guess I got a sense of the history of the modern world through these stories, albeit a racist and stereotypical and ethnocentric one. But still...

Once I was walking to school and I passed a quilt lying in the garbage. When I came home later in the day, the same quilt had been washed and ironed and folded at the foot of my bed. He told me he had paid good money for it at an auction in Old Montreal.

I have a shelf filled with absurd objects that my dad gave me as gifts. My friends will often stop in front of it and say something along the lines of, "Why the hell do you have this shelf of worthless and tacky shit?" At which point I will often explain the origins of these articles, how each one was given to me by my father when he would come to visit. Then they think of them as beautiful. The ceramic goose with a top hat suddenly seems quite debonair, and begins to tell a tale about its childhood outside Berlin.

WHEN HE WAS YOUNG, my dad had been a great criminal.
He was very proud of these years. Not having pursued a life
of crime was his greatest regret, I think. He wished he could
have been one of the gangsters that Martin Scorsese made
movies about. He thought their lives were wonderful. They
had escaped their class with a vengeance, exacting a reck-
oning on everyone who had belittled them, and then
everyone else, just for good measure. What was there not to
love? We watched every gangster film many times.

My dad believed that, under certain circumstances, breaking
the law was not a great moral dilemma. He definitely had a
lax view about stealing, because he did it all the time.

As a child, I was crazy about cheese. So in the evenings my
father would stop at select grocery stores to steal the most
expensive cheese on display. At home, he would arrange the
cheese in cubes on a plate that was covered in a pattern of
rabbits: blue cheese, camembert, gruyère. He would pronounce
them in funny ways because he couldn't read really well. He
would bring out the plate while we were watching television,

and we would eat them with frilly toothpicks. We'd turn from the episode of *The Benny Hill Show* and nod at each other whenever the mouthful was particularly delightful.

I think no one would argue that if a parent steals for a child, they should not be convicted of anything at all. This is a crime driven by necessity. It is almost a duty to commit such a crime. However, would one argue that it is necessary to steal outrageously expensive cheese for one's child when said child has developed a taste for such?

I developed a taste for very expensive cheese. My father said my taste in cheese showed I was refined. It proved I was a French aristocrat. He continued to steal delicacies from the supermarket for me throughout my childhood.

"Caviar, milady!" He said one night, pulling a tiny jar out of his left pocket.

"Ooooh!" I declared.

From out of his other pocket, he pulled a box of tiny marzipan apples. What could I do but applaud and throw my arms around his neck?

By the end of his life, we would have to travel a mile by city bus before he could go to a grocery store. He had been banned from all the ones in the neighbourhood. Nobody was going to put you in jail for stealing a fancy imported bottle of olive oil for your child, but they would bar you from ever returning again.

The take-away from this was that I should not settle for what was offered to me in life. I should want more than what my father could afford. And I was expected to find methods other than stealing to get them.

LESSON 9 | *Enjoy a Fondue Dinner*

WE ALWAYS WENT to Warshaw's to go shopping. It was a giant family-run grocery store. They don't really have them anymore. You used to be able to fall in love with a grocery store. In the back there was always a shelf of random items for sale: tea sets, woks, flower pots, etc. They were always offered at cut-throat prices.

One afternoon, we chanced upon a fondue pot. My dad held it up. This was it. Now there was no difference between us and millionaires. If we were eating fondue, then we were eating like King Henry the Eighth. No way around it. He bought the fondue pot since he couldn't exactly fit it in his pocket.

For the next week, my dad began to make preparations for our fondue dinner. He decided to invite all our loved ones over, because there is no point in going through the trouble of having a fondue dinner without inviting loads of people to share in it. My dad hated his biological family with a passion, so none of them were invited. He called up all his friends.

My dad's friends were an eclectic bunch. He had a friend who had robbed a bank and had served eleven years in prison. The friend had promised to take care of his friend's handicapped daughter, and he kept his word. He was very mild-mannered and was always on his way to the store with a grocery cart. He kept to his mundane tasks all day. He taught me about how you can remake your life at any time. And how true goodness came from unexpected sources.

There was a rather bright man named Sylvain. I adored him. He was skinny and he had a lovely way of speaking. He wore a suit and would often have a flower on his lapel. He reminded me of people from PBS shows. He would drink and start to laugh and weep. His moods were rollercoasters. They were Shakespearian tragedies. His flights of fancy were a primer for understanding Shakespeare and some of the work I did at McGill.

There was a young black man named Percival. He used to walk around the city all day to calm his nerves. He walked as though it were a job. Animals liked him. He would speak to our toy poodle in such a high-pitched voice that it would actually faint from joy. He could whistle like all kinds of birds. Since I lived downtown, I didn't know what any bird other than a pigeon sounded like. But the noises he made were beautiful just the same. He was a modern-day Kierkegaard. He really could have written *Fear and Trembling*, a treatise on existential anxiety and the terrifying responsibility of choice.

Was it because I read a lot as a kid that I had the literary skills to appreciate these characters? Or was it those characters who caused me to read books in a different way? It was probably an intersection of both.

They all came to our fondue dinner. My dad went to great lengths to prepare the meal that night. There was no cooking feat that was beyond my dad's power. We would stand in front of the photographs of dishes in the windows of Chinese restaurants, studying them as though they were paintings in a gallery. Then he would go home and replicate the dishes. He would purchase yellow boxes of MSG at the Chinese grocery store and dump them into sauces. Food rarely tastes like anything at all to me now.

He made elaborate desserts too, champagne glasses with Jell-O and whipped cream, ice cream cones with cupcakes inside. My dad bought giant jars of maraschino cherries wholesale. He made shortbread cookies and ordered me about as I helped him. He looked more like he was a member of the Hell's Angels cutting up a brick of hash than a parent making cookies for a child.

After getting the meal ready, he went to get dressed. He had a closet of suits. He was very proud of them because they had all been purchased hot. For him the mark of a fine suit was that it had been stolen. Suits that were purchased at a store were cheap. But the ones you stole were of top-notch quality.

Our guests arrived one by one. My dad somehow thought you could only eat fondue in the dark, as though it were a campfire to scare away miniscule wolves. Because we had to wait until the sun went down, they started drinking on

Heather O'Neill

empty stomachs. And then they started going completely insane.

They started feeling sorry for themselves. And when men who are over fifty and have nothing to show for their efforts begin to feel sorry for themselves, mayhem ensues. They started setting their money on fire. They started singing and arm wrestling and falling down stairs. Percival ended up outside yelling in the middle of the street that no one loved him.

"Ignore him," my dad said, as I dipped the bread into the cheese.

All in all, it was a great night. Everyone had an opportunity to pontificate and articulate their rage and existential concerns. Everyone had a chance to declare that love was a sham. Ex-wives were toasted sarcastically. Threats to enemies were made. Religion was condemned. Universal outrage was the order of the day. It was, in other words, just another night in the Court of Henry the Eighth.

And the word "fondue" still makes me happy.

MY DAD HAD ALL SORTS OF IDEAS about what family was
and none had to do with biology. A family is a group of
trusted associates. Most importantly, a family is a group of
people who take each other seriously, and who are interested
in one another's perspectives.

My dad was always telling me people were related to me.
He would introduce me to someone and give them the title
"cousin." Matthew was one of my many uncles. These terms
were earned through merit and not blood.

One day Matthew told my father that a young woman
had moved in with him. She was very beautiful. She kept him
up all night wanting to dance in the kitchen and have drinks.
She wore a yellow dress that he liked, and it spun out when
she danced. She insisted he compliment her all the time. But
despite all the difficulties she brought with her, it was better
than living alone.

My dad told me we should go over and see what was what.

I loved going over to his apartment anyways. He had been
living in the apartment for so long that the rent was only

two hundred and some dollars. It still had the furnishings of a 1940s home. It was decorated during a time before rampant consumerism, before everything lost its beauty and meaning days after you brought it. Each room had a different style of wallpaper, the kind that you just don't see any more, with patterns that depicted exquisite worlds of flowers and delicate birds. There were framed photos of him when he was younger. It was hard to imagine that he lived in a time where everyone was black and white and listened to old-timey music.

The only things that were strange or modern were all the Pepsi bottles that filled up the backyard. There were hundreds of them back there. One night when it hailed, the noise of the ice pellets on the bottles played Stravinsky's *Rite of Spring*. But only the black cats were there to testify.

We sat in the kitchen and ate chopped-up hotdogs on exquisite plates. We drank Pepsi out of teacups the shape of open lilies that seemed as though they must close at night and be covered in drops of dew in the morning.

After eating, he suddenly looked up, and pointed to the hallways. "She's up!" he said. I followed him to the back of the house. There were rooms that he kept closed off to visitors. He opened the door to the parlour carefully. He pointed to the wingback chair with its blue roses in the middle of the room. I stared at the empty chair for a moment.

"Hello," I said.

"She's lovely isn't she?" Matthew exclaimed.

She was indeed the most beautiful woman that anyone had ever seen.

Older people are eccentric, but they are the best, I discovered then. Their homes are filled with objects that are so infused with nostalgia, they are practically alive. They have wonderful rich inner lives that are replete with wisdom and magic realism. They weave the past into the present. They remember odd details from other eras that you can't find in history books. I was glad my dad introduced me to so many as a child.

I feel that I need to pause for a moment and interrupt this train of thought—just in case you're getting the idea that my dad was this wonderful guy. Full disclosure: he was an asshole. There's no way around it. His behaviour was pretty shocking. He was the kind of guy who would be watering the grass, then turn the hose on someone walking by, thus instigating a fistfight.

My father would always brag about the bar fights he had gotten into as a young man. He claimed that the most underrated weapon in the world is the ketchup bottle. It is inconspicuous in your hand and creates high drama when it is smashed against someone's head.

In the interest of journalistic integrity, I thought I'd put that out there.

LESSON 11 | *It's the Thought That Counts*

MY DAD USED TO give me cheques for my birthday. They would be for enormous amounts that dazzled me. Once he gave me a cheque for a hundred dollars. The only thing was that he wouldn't sign them. He said that he didn't have the funds in his account right at the moment, but he would sign it as soon as he did. I collected the cheques in a vinyl wallet in my underwear drawer, certain that one day I would be a millionaire, as they were really adding up.

They represented not what he could give me, but what he wanted to give me.

There was always another less spectacular, unassuming gift as well. One year, he bought me a copy of *Anne of Green Gables* for my birthday. I don't know why he thought I would like it. Maybe a store owner suggested it to him, or maybe a girlfriend.

I read it and was madly in love with Anne Shirley. I was angry that the book was over. I was upset with her. I thought

I would be miserable for the rest of my life now because every girl would fall short, compared to Anne Shirley. I didn't like that other people were able to read *Anne of Green Gables*. None of the other readers loved her the way I did. I wanted what we had to be exclusive. If she was a real person, she would have had to file a restraining order against me. I reread the book almost immediately after finishing it.

I saw on the back of the book that there were other titles in the collection. I asked my dad if he would buy me the next one. It was rather obnoxious because my birthday had just passed and I was asking for something else. But to my surprise and delight, my father immediately said, "Yes." We took the bus to the bookstore downtown. We found the books on the shelf, and my dad bought not one, but every title in the series. The cashier put all eight books in a paper bag. I carried them in my arms on the way home. I never wanted to be separated from them.

This is one of my loveliest memories. But did he really know what he was getting into? He should have known then that there was something wrong with the way I read. The same way you can tell when there is something wrong with the way someone drinks, say.

Over the next few years, I began to read in a desperate, wild, brave, obsessive manner. People associate reading with doing homework and being good at school. But that's the ordinary kind of reader. That's not the type of reading that I'm talking about. I'm talking about extreme reading. Reading stuff that doesn't make sense, the degenerate intellectuals, the off-Broadway playwrights, German postwar melancholia of inherited guilt, the Edwardian snobs, the treatises on public toilets written by 1960s homosexuals.

I also began writing more and more. Since he couldn't curb my journaling, my dad suggested that I might record his advice and pass it on to others afterwards. Perhaps if I were to write a book it could be called *The Pensées of Buddy O'Neill*. And that it could be the foundation of a universal school of thought, like Scientology.

But my writing began to be its own monster. My professors were always surprised at my prolific writings, because I just seemed like a white trash girl destined to work at a Dunkin' Donuts and give birth to juvenile delinquents. But I was reading all the time, thinking about any philosophy that I could get my hands on, and interpreting texts. I was developing an odd aesthetic that incorporated my childhood reality and the high art of literary fiction. You might not agree with these analogies, but I was going for this:

- A cross between Marguerite Duras and a used-car salesman;
- A mix of *Satyricon* and a McDonald's Birthday Party;
- Isabel Archer as a 1970s Las Vegas underage showgirl;
- Percy Shelley explaining to a court why he can't afford child support;
- Agatha Christie and the paranoid lady on the ground floor who was involved in everyone's business;
- Hunter S. Thompson and the little kid on the Big Wheel who went around and around the block with a big attitude;

- Samuel Beckett and the couple that fought all the time threatening to kill each other then sat down for tea;
- Jean Rhys if she worked in a peep show booth on St. Laurent Boulevard and when you put a coin in the slot and the door went up, she would be sitting there naked and frowning and not following any of your instructions. And she made you cry;
- A cross between Antonin Artaud's Theatre of Cruelty and the cast of *The Muppet Show*;
- Lewis Carroll and late-night news anchors who are always laughing when the camera comes back to them;
- George Bataille and a skipping-rope chant;
- Vladimir Nabokov and the doll section of the Hudson's Bay department store;
- Ralph Ellison and all the lamps my dad took out of the garbage;
- Words of wisdom from a Bazooka Joe comic and Friedrich Nietzsche;
- Margaret Atwood and my absent mother.

Although I was clearly leaving my dad behind intellectually, it was he who had given me, in part, the confidence to think of my life as being worthy to mix with those of the geniuses.

LESSON 12 | *Never Watch a Paul Newman Movie*

MY DAD SAID that he didn't care how many people said that Paul Newman was a good actor, this wasn't the case at all.

My dad talked about Paul Newman as though Paul Newman had stolen his life. My dad had been quite handsome when he was young, but he hadn't been able to trade on being good looking. Furthermore, my dad said that his own salad dressing was the very best in the world. He steamed the label off old bottles of Paul Newman salad dressing and filled them with a perfect mixture of oil and vinegar and spices. But he hadn't made a cent off it. Where was the justice?

My dad thought of himself and Paul Newman as having been switched at birth. He ranted about it any time Newman appeared in a late-night movie.

The way that my dad talked about Paul Newman made it seem as though they must know each other. Only a long-term grievance could motivate this type of rancour. For a period in my life, I thought that Paul Newman was from Montreal. And that he had grown up on St. Urbain Street and had gone to Baron Byng High School.

I always assumed he must have picked on my dad in school.

I kept expecting Paul Newman to pop up in family photos. I didn't really understand that American movie stars lived in New York or Hollywood. I thought that they all just lived downtown, near where all the multiplex movie theatres were.

Sometimes the doorbell would ring out of the blue and I would be terrified that it was Paul Newman at the door, come to stir things up, come to open old wounds. Or that we might run into Paul Newman at the Canada Day parade, eating red-and-white cake with a plastic spoon and that all hell would break loose.

Whenever I brought up that Paul Newman was a terrible actor, my friends' parents looked at me, completely shocked. They had a look on their face as though they didn't know who I was.

But my dad and I would hold up our ginger ale glasses and clink them together: "Not to Paul Newman," we would toast.

There was a repertory cinema near my house. My dad was friends with the guy who ran it, so he would get me free tickets to see any movie I liked. Then one afternoon when I was thirteen, I saw the movie *The Hustler* which, unbeknownst to me, starred Paul Newman. There I was in the darkness with

Paul Newman. He was so charming and tortured, clever and hapless.

How could I not love him?

Perhaps my dad thought that if he could keep me away from Paul Newman, he could keep me away from the knowledge that he and every child acquires once they grow up, that they aren't the most spectacular and lovable person on earth after all.

I didn't tell him that I thought that Paul Newman was a wonderful actor. I was the one person in the world who believed that he was better than Paul Newman. I have still, however, never tried his salad dressing out of respect for my father.

I WAS HAPPY AS A CHILD. And, although I liked having an absurd rule book to follow, most of my favourite times with my dad happened when he wasn't giving me any advice at all. All those wonderful days when we would totally forget about everything and decide to be the happy losers that we were.

We would go to the La Fontaine Park zoo. We would feed peanuts to the deer. My dad said the piglets were so cute, he would put one in his inside pocket for me one day and take it home. One of the main attractions was a baby elephant. When it crapped, we would applaud happily.

We always went to sit in St. Louis Square. There was one time when my dad bought us both a pile of clothes from a menswear store that was going out of business. So picture us both wearing our headbands and our tweed suits, eating sandwiches like old men. There was something about that park that appealed to both of us. We were always in a good mood when we were in the park. There was something like a never-never land about it, filled with drug addicts and bohemians.

There were heroin addicts everywhere. They didn't seem alarming to me as a child. They had expressions like cartoon characters that had just been hit on the head with a frying pan. They seemed harmless, especially since they did things in slow motion. For instance, it might take one an hour to tie their shoe. They'd bend down to tie it and get stuck there. They slept everywhere. They reminded me of toddlers who fell asleep regularly and at the drop of a hat.

My dad didn't warn me about doing drugs or about drug addicts. It seemed so much a part of the fabric of our lives that to stay away from junkies was absurd. If we shut out people who had addictions, then who would we spend time with, and where was the fun in that?

But the park was filled with another threat. St. Louis Square and Prince Arthur Street were a hubbub of street performers back then. I went mad for the clowns, and plopped myself down in front of each to better consume their spectacle. There was a clown who wept so hard he would wipe the tears off his face with a sponge and then squeeze it out on the sidewalk. There was a clown who played "Habanera" from *Carmen* on a Chiclets container. There was a ballerina with a red nose who had a small stage shaped like a jewellery box that she spun around on. There was a clown who fired a gun at his head and a burst of confetti drifted gently over the crowd like snow.

Although he didn't warn me about drug addicts, my dad spent plenty of time warning me about clowns. I always thought of clowns as moralists who acknowledged that every mundane moment of the day was painful. How could they not be, given that the world was filled with tragedy and despair.

My dad thought they were people who didn't want to get jobs, who panhandled from children.

Once there was a woman who stood in the path leading up to the flower kiosk, which was a natural performance space. She had black hair that looked as though she had just woken up—bedhead as the fashion stylists like to call it— and wore a small black cotton dress with a white collar. She looked like Edith Piaf! She was accompanied by an extremely handsome accordion player. Until then, I had thought of accordion players as old men, who had small dogs tied to the legs of the kitchen chairs they performed on outside the grocery store. But this accordionist was black and young and fit and was dressed in a pinstriped suit and brand-new shoes.

She would sing a few lines. Then she would stop to complain to the accordion player that he wasn't getting it right. They would produce the most lovely seconds of music and then stop to squabble. It was as though they were arguing in the living room of their own house. They seemed to be lovers, because they exhibited the traits of people who knew each other too well. I wished that they would just accept one another's flaws and play. But who knows, perhaps it was all part of the act. Maybe the performers had made a deliberate choice to add Brechtian interruptions. They were taking life apart and understanding it as art, seeing every moment of it, no matter how crude and cheap, as being worthy of profound examination.

I was not ashamed of myself, or the way my father was, which was what made me an artist and not a criminal.

Most of all, I think my father believed that if clowns wooed me away, the whole world would woo me away from him, too. And what in the world did he have other than me? He had had three wives who had all left him. He had other children he rarely saw. Maybe he thought I would disappear and leave him the way that everybody else left him. But I didn't. I don't know why, but I loved him the most.

CODA | *Sometimes There Is Nothing to Be Learned*

ALTHOUGH I BROKE ALL THE RULES that my dad gave me, they gave me a context for life. They made life seem exciting. They gave me a sense that everything I did was important, and I have carried that notion through my life.

When he was dying, a nurse came over to the apartment to visit. "I don't think your father is taking his pills," he said.

"You're wrong," I said. "Of course he's taking his pills. They get delivered to the door from the pharmacy every week."

After the nurse left, I started looking through the drawers and cabinets. And behind one cupboard door in the kitchen I discovered all his pill boxes neatly stacked one on top of the other, with their seals unbroken. They resembled a small urban skyline at dusk.

"Dad!" I said. "What are all the pills doing here? You're supposed to take them."

"Quick!" he yelled, putting his arms up in the air so I'd help him out of bed. "Let's get rid of them before the nurse comes back!"

We dumped the bottles of pills into the toilet one by one. It was like we were in a Martin Scorsese picture and the feds were at the door, and we had to dispose of all the bags of cocaine. There was something oddly pleasant about the afternoon. We were back to breaking the law again. We were back to being master criminals. We outwitted everyone until the very end. We were gangsters after all.

‖ In heaven I'll probably find another version of St. Louis Square. But in that park, the French-Canadian Edith Piaf will finally launch into her song, and the accordion player will not be frustrated. And they will play the tune that immortal people with no worries play. And in that park the baby elephant will sit on my lap and blow its trunk and perform a slow tuba solo. And then the elephant will take a dump, and we will all applaud.

And in that park, my father will be sitting on a bench, waiting for me, with a pen out. Ready to sign all the birthday cheques.

ADVICE FROM YOUR OWN FATHER

When I was little, and my father had great authority, I lived in a magical world created in part by his morals and maps.

Childhood is a time when we listen to our parents as though they are the wisest people on earth. But then, some of the things they teach us are absolutely ridiculous or just plain misguided.

I invite you to record some of the lessons your own parents or mentors taught you in the following pages: the good ones and the bad ones, because their words, for better or worse, are unforgettable.

ADVICE FROM YOUR OWN FATHER

ADVICE FROM YOUR OWN FATHER

CLC KREISEL LECTURE SERIES